United States Presidents

Zachary Taylor

Paul Joseph
ABDO Publishing Company

visit us at
www.abdopub.com

Published by Abdo Publishing Company 4940 Viking Drive, Edina, Minnesota 55435.
Copyright © 1999 by Abdo Consulting Group, Inc. International copyrights reserved in
all countries. No part of this book may be reproduced in any form without written
permission from the publisher.

Printed in the United States.

Cover and Interior Photo credits: AP/Wide World, Archive, Corbis-Bettmann

Contributing editors: Robert Italia, Tamara L. Britton, K. M. Brielmaier
Book design/maps: Patrick Laurel

Library of Congress Cataloging-in-Publication Data

Joseph, Paul, 1970-
    Zachary Taylor / Paul Joseph.
        p. cm. -- (United States presidents)
    Includes index.
    Summary: Presents a biography of "Old Rough and Ready," hero of
the Mexican War, who became the twelfth president of the United
States.
    ISBN 1-57765-233-9
        1. Taylor, Zachary, 1784-1850--Juvenile literature.
    2. Presidents -- United States -- Biography -- Juvenile Literature.
    [1. Taylor, Zachary, 1784-1850. 2. Presidents.] I. Title.
    II. Series: United States presidents (Edina, Minn.)
    E422.J67 1999
    973.6'3'092--dc21
        [B]   98-14588
                                                            CIP
Revised Edition 2002   AC

Contents

Zachary Taylor

Zachary Taylor was the twelfth president of the United States. Taylor had no political experience. But he spent 40 years in the military serving the country. He was a good leader.

Taylor was elected president in 1848. At that time, Americans were arguing over slavery. Taylor owned more than 100 slaves. But he did not believe that new states should have slavery.

The Southern states were not happy with Taylor. They wanted new states to allow slavery. The South began talking about leaving the Union. President Taylor never saw the end of the struggle over slavery. On July 9, 1850, he died.

Opposite page:
A rare photo of
Zachary Taylor

Zachary Taylor (1784-1850)
Twelfth President

BORN:	November 24, 1784
PLACE OF BIRTH:	Montebello, Orange County, Virginia
ANCESTRY:	English
FATHER:	Richard Taylor (1744-1829)
MOTHER:	Sarah Dabney Strother Taylor (1760-1822)
WIFE:	Margaret Mackall Smith (1788-1852)
CHILDREN:	Six: 1 boy, 5 girls
EDUCATION:	Private tutors
RELIGION:	Episcopalian
OCCUPATION:	Soldier, farmer
MILITARY SERVICE:	Volunteer in Kentucky Militia (1803); rose from first lieutenant to major general in U.S. Army (1808-1849)
POLITICAL PARTY:	Whig

OFFICES HELD:	None
AGE AT INAUGURATION:	64
YEARS SERVED:	1849-1850
VICE PRESIDENT:	Millard Fillmore
DIED:	July 9, 1850, Washington, D.C., age 65
CAUSE OF DEATH:	Gastroenteritis

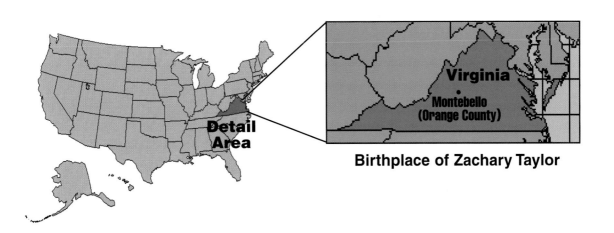

Detail Area

Virginia

Montebello
(Orange County)

Birthplace of Zachary Taylor

Young Zachary

Zachary Taylor was born in Montebello, Orange County, Virginia, on November 24, 1784. He was the third of nine children born to Richard and Sarah Taylor.

Zachary's parents came from wealthy families. Richard was a **lieutenant colonel** in the **American Revolution**. Sarah was well educated. She received her schooling from **tutors**.

A few months after Zachary was born, the family moved into what is now northern Kentucky. Zachary grew up on his father's **plantation** in Jefferson County.

The family was very close. Zachary's brothers and sisters were his only friends. A tutor taught the Taylor children at home.

Richard told his children stories about the American Revolution. Zachary decided he wanted to be in the military. So did most of his brothers. All but one joined the army. Zachary became one of the most famous military men in U.S. history.

The United States (1790)

New
Hampshire

Republic of
Vermont

Massachusetts

New York

Rhode Island

Connecticut

Pennsylvania

New Jersey

Maryland

Delaware

Spanish Territory

Northwest
Territory

Virginia

North
Carolina

Southwest
Territory

South
Carolina

Georgia

Land Claimed by
Spain and the U.S.

Military and Family

Zachary Taylor joined the army in 1808 as a **lieutenant**. In 1810, he became a **captain**. He also married Margaret Mackall Smith. Margaret was born in Calvert County, Maryland, in 1788.

The Taylors had five daughters and one son. Two daughters, Octavia and Margaret, died before age three. Their son Richard served as a lieutenant in the **Confederate** army. Their three remaining daughters, Ann, Sarah, and Mary Elizabeth, married military men.

On June 17, 1835, Sarah married Jefferson Davis. Davis was in the army. Later, he served in **Congress** as a representative from Mississippi. When the South left the Union and formed the Confederate States of America, Davis was the president of this new country.

Mary Elizabeth married Colonel William Bliss. She would act as White House hostess after her father became president of the United States.

Zachary Taylor's daughter, Mary Elizabeth Taylor Bliss

A Great War Leader

*I*n the **War of 1812**, Taylor became a **major**. He served at frontier posts along the Mississippi River. He became a **lieutenant colonel** in 1819. By 1832, Taylor was a popular and respected **colonel**.

Taylor wore a plain uniform. Although he was a high-ranking officer, Taylor usually fought in battles. Many times he was close to enemy fire. His men gave him the nickname Old Rough and Ready.

In 1837, Taylor defeated the **Seminoles** at Lake Okeechobee, Florida. Because of his victory, Taylor was made a **brigadier general**. In 1840, Taylor became the commander at Fort Smith, Arkansas, then at Fort Jesup, Louisiana.

The United States **annexed** Texas in 1845. It became a state that year. The U.S. also claimed that the boundary between Mexico and Texas was a river called the Rio Grande.

Texas and Mexico in 1846

The Mexican government was angry. They claimed that the boundary was the Nueces River. The two countries prepared for war. In 1846, President James Polk sent Taylor to Texas. He set up a military base near the Rio Grande.

The Mexican-American War began on May 13, 1846. Taylor and his soldiers entered Mexico. Taylor and his men captured the city of Monterrey.

In 1847, the Mexican army attacked Taylor and his men at Buena Vista. Taylor's army was outnumbered. But they won the battle. The victory made Taylor an American hero.

The Making of the Twelfth United States President

 **1784**

Born November 24 in Montebello, Orange County, Virginia

 **1785**

The family moves to northern Kentucky

 **1808**

Begins serving as first lieutenant in the army

 **1819**

Becomes a lieutenant colonel

 1832

Colonel in Black Hawk War

 1837

Defeats the Seminole Indians in the Battle of Lake Okeechobee, Florida

 1845

Texas is annexed

1846

Commander of many battles during Mexican-American War

1847

Battle of Buena Vista

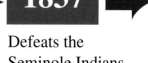 **1848**

Mexican-American war ends; elected president of the United States

Zachary Taylor

"For more than half a century . . . this Union has stood unshaken. . . .
Whatever dangers may threaten it, I shall stand by it and maintain its integrity. . . . "

1810

Becomes a
captain; marries
Margaret Smith

1812

Major in the
War of 1812

Historic Events
during Taylor's Presidency

★ Gold rush to California

★ *David Copperfield* by
Charles Dickens is published

★ The world's first underwater cable is
laid in the Atlantic Ocean between
England and France

1838

Promoted to
brigadier
general

1840

Commander at Fort
Smith, Arkansas

1849

Congress debates
Clay's compromise

1850

Dies on July 9

1850

Congress passes
the Compromise
of 1850

PRESIDENTIAL   YEARS

Back to the Plantation

*I*n 1847, Taylor returned to his Louisiana **plantation**. Many Americans thought Taylor should run for president. But Taylor was content to stay home and farm.

The Mexican-American War ended in 1848. Mexico had to give the United States thousands of square miles of land. This land was known as the Mexican Cession.

Northern **representative** David Wilmot suggested a new law called the Wilmot Proviso. It would forbid slavery in the new territory.

The Wilmot Proviso was popular in the North. But it never became law. Southern senators voted against it. The South wanted slavery in the new territory.

The United States
(1850)

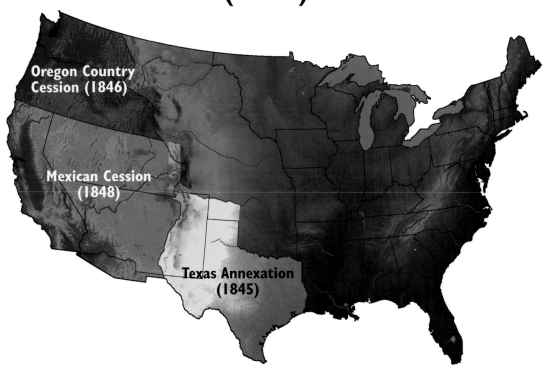

Oregon Country
Cession (1846)

Mexican Cession
(1848)

Texas Annexation
(1845)

The Election of 1848

*T*he 1848 election for president approached. Taylor was not interested in seeking election. But he said he would run for president if people wanted him to.

The **Democratic** party chose Senator Lewis Cass of Michigan to run for president. Cass felt that the **settlers** in the new territory should decide if they wanted slavery.

Many Northern Democrats wanted to end slavery. They were known as Free-Soilers. They even started their own political party. They called it the Free-Soil Party. They chose former president Martin Van Buren to run for president.

The Democratic party was divided. So, the **Whig party** felt they could win the election. They chose Zachary Taylor to run for president. Millard Fillmore was their choice for vice president.

Taylor campaigned very hard. He reminded voters of his military record. He promised that his **administration** would be made of people from all over America.

Taylor rarely talked about slavery. He was a Southerner. He owned more than 100 slaves. In November 1848, Taylor was elected the twelfth president of the United States.

Vice President
Millard Fillmore

The Twelfth President

*A*fter the election, President Taylor voiced his views on slavery. He believed that people in the South should be allowed to keep their slaves. But he also believed that new territories and states should not allow slavery.

Southerners were not happy. Some Southern leaders wanted the South to become a new country. But President Taylor did not want the South to leave the Union.

There also were problems in Texas, a slave state. Texas **militiamen** threatened to drive the U.S. Army out of Santa Fe. As president, Taylor was commander-in-chief of the military. He warned that he would lead the U.S. Army against the militiamen and hang any traitors. The Texas **revolt** never happened.

Opposite page:
President
Zachary Taylor

More slavery problems appeared. President Taylor wanted the California and New Mexico territories to join the Union as free states. But some Southern congressman wanted slavery allowed in California.

Whig senator Henry Clay of Kentucky presented ideas to **Congress** about the slavery problem. Clay thought it would be good for America if some new states allowed slavery. He wanted the New Mexico and Utah territories to become slave states. His ideas were called Clay's compromise.

President Taylor would not support Clay's compromise. He stood firm against new slave states.

The slavery **debate** continued. Northern and Southern senators argued with each other. Sometimes, fistfights broke out. It seemed the slavery problem would never be solved.

Opposite page:
Whig senator
Henry Clay

The Seven "Hats" of the U.S. President

A president can serve only two terms. Each term lasts four years. When Taylor was president, this law did not exist.

A president is elected or re-elected every four years.

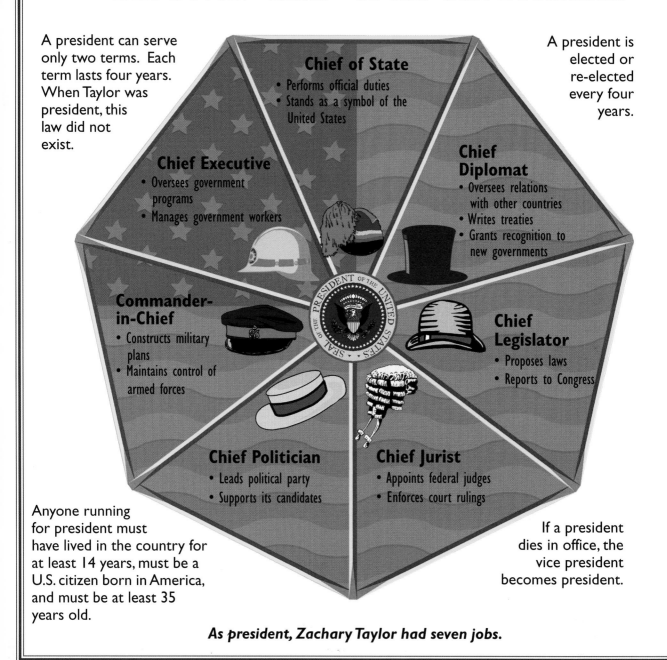

Chief of State
- Performs official duties
- Stands as a symbol of the United States

Chief Executive
- Oversees government programs
- Manages government workers

Chief Diplomat
- Oversees relations with other countries
- Writes treaties
- Grants recognition to new governments

Commander-in-Chief
- Constructs military plans
- Maintains control of armed forces

Chief Legislator
- Proposes laws
- Reports to Congress

Chief Politician
- Leads political party
- Supports its candidates

Chief Jurist
- Appoints federal judges
- Enforces court rulings

Anyone running for president must have lived in the country for at least 14 years, must be a U.S. citizen born in America, and must be at least 35 years old.

If a president dies in office, the vice president becomes president.

As president, Zachary Taylor had seven jobs.

The Three Branches of the U.S. Government

Congress is in the Capitol Building in Washington, D.C. It can pass laws and stop the president's veto. Congress also can change the Constitution to stop the president's plans or Supreme Court rulings.

The president lives in the White House in Washington, D.C. He or she can stop (veto) laws passed by Congress, and propose new laws. The president also can choose Supreme Court judges.

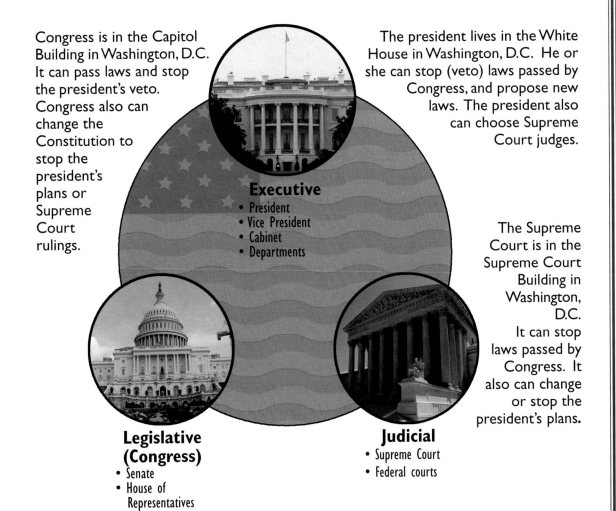

Executive
- President
- Vice President
- Cabinet
- Departments

The Supreme Court is in the Supreme Court Building in Washington, D.C. It can stop laws passed by Congress. It also can change or stop the president's plans.

Legislative (Congress)
- Senate
- House of Representatives

Judicial
- Supreme Court
- Federal courts

The U.S. Constitution formed three government branches. Each branch has power over the others. So, no single group or person can control the country. The Constitution calls this "separation of powers."

President Taylor Dies

*O*n July 4, 1850, President Taylor attended a Fourth of July picnic in Washington, D.C. That evening, he became sick. He stayed in bed for five days. But he did not get better. On July 9, 1850, President Taylor died. He was in office for only 16 months.

The slavery **debate** continued. Two months later, Senator Clay's ideas about slavery became law. This law was called the Compromise of 1850.

Taylor served his country for more than 40 years. He was a successful army leader. As president, he took a firm stand against the spread of slavery in America. President Taylor is buried in Louisville, Kentucky, in the Zachary Taylor National Cemetery.

The Compromise of 1850

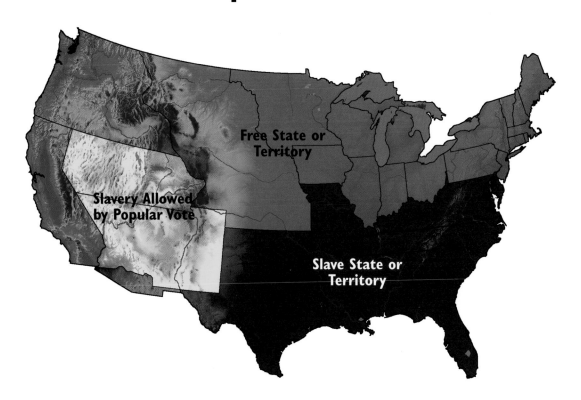

Free State or Territory

Slavery Allowed by Popular Vote

Slave State or Territory

Fun Facts

- President Taylor moved around so much as a military man, he never had an official place to call home. Because of that, he never voted in any election, not even his own.

- President Taylor's old war-horse, Whitey, lived on the White House grounds. Visitors pulled hairs from his tail for souvenirs.

- Taylor's legs were so short, he had to be helped onto his horse.

Opposite page:
Taylor and his
horse, Whitey

Glossary

administration - the people in charge of running the government.

American Revolution - 1775-1783. A war between Great Britain and its colonies in America. The Americans won their independence and created the United States.

annex - when a country is taken over by another country.

brigadier general - a one-star general.

captain - a military rank above lieutenant and below major.

colonel - a military rank above major and below brigadier general.

Confederacy - the 11 Southern states that left the Union between 1860 and 1861.

Congress - the lawmaking body of the U.S. government. It is made up of the House of Representatives and the Senate.

debate - a public talk about topics or questions.

Democrat - one of the two main political parties in the United States. Democrats are often more liberal and believe in more government.

lieutenant - a military rank above sergeant and below captain.

lieutenant colonel - a military rank above major and below colonel.

major - a military rank above captain and below colonel.

militiamen - citizens trained for war or emergencies. The National Guard.

plantation - a huge farm that grows crops such as tobacco, cotton, or sugar cane.

representative - a person who is elected by the people to represent a certain area. Representatives make laws in Washington, D.C., and are part of the House of Representatives.

revolt - when a group of people refuse to follow the government.

Seminoles - a group of Native Americans who live in Florida.

settlers - people who move to a new land and build a community.

tutor - a private teacher.

War of 1812 - a war between America and Great Britain over shipping and sailors' rights.

Whig party - a political party that was very strong in the early 1800s, but ended in the 1850s. They supported laws that favored business.

Internet Sites

PBS American Presidents Series
http://www.americanpresidents.org
Visit the PBS Web site which features the biographies of each president. Check out the key events of each presidency, speeches, fun facts, and trivia games.

Welcome to the White House
http://www.whitehouse.gov
The official Web site of the White House. After an introduction from the current president of the United States, the site takes you through biographies of each president. Get information on White House history, art in the White House, first ladies, first families, and much more.

POTUS—Presidents of the United States
http://www.ipl.org/ref/POTUS/
In this Web site you will find background information, election results, cabinet members, presidency highlights, and some odd facts on each of the presidents. Links to biographies, historical documents, audio and video files, and other presidential sites are also included to enrich this site.

These sites are subject to change. Go to your favorite search engine and type in United States presidents for more sites.

Pass It On

History enthusiasts: educate readers around the country by passing on information you've learned about presidents or other important people who have changed history. Share your little-known facts and interesting stories. We want to hear from you!

To get posted on the ABDO Publishing Company Web site, email us at "History@abdopub.com"
Visit the ABDO Publishing Company Web site at www.abdopub.com

Index